W9-DGM-619

IOLI KALAVREZOU-MAXEINER

BYZANTINE ICONS IN STEATITE

BYZANTINA VINDOBONENSIA
Herausgegeben von der Kommission
für frühchristliche und ostkirchliche Kunst der Österreichischen Akademie
der Wissenschaften und vom Institut für Byzantinistik und Neogräzistik
der Universität Wien

BAND XV/2

IOLI KALAVREZOU-MAXEINER

BYZANTINE ICONS IN STEATITE

With 4 Color Plates
and 96 Plates in Black and White

PLATES

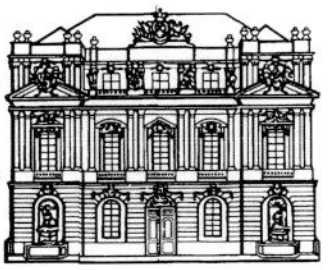

VERLAG
DER ÖSTERREICHISCHEN AKADEMIE DER WISSENSCHAFTEN
WIEN 1985

Vorgelegt von w. M. OTTO DEMUS in der Sitzung am 15. Dezember 1982

Gedruckt mit Unterstützung durch das
Bundesministerium für Wissenschaft und Forschung

— ISBN 3 7001 0682 3

Druck: Ernst Becvar, A-1150 Wien

LIST OF ILLUSTRATIONS

No. 39 Washington, D.C., Dumbarton Oaks, *Head of Saint*
No. 40 Location Unknown, *Head of Saint*
No. 41 Cherson, Museum, *Annunciation*
No. 42 Istanbul, Archaeological Museum, *Annunciation*
No. 43 Leningrad, Hermitage, *Virgin Enthroned*
No. 44 New York, Metropolitan Museum, *Crucifixion*
No. 45 Leningrad, Hermitage, *Crucifixion and Entombment*
No. 46 Syracuse, Palace of Archbishop, *Staurotheque*
No. 47 Paris, Cabinet des Médailles, *Staurotheque*
No. 48 Thasos, Museum, *Deesis*
No. 49 Baltimore, Walters Art Gallery, *Crucifixion* (?)
No. 50 New York, Metropolitan Museum, *Presentation in the Temple*
No. 51 Toronto, University of Toronto, *Saints*
No. 52 Toledo, Cathedral Treasury, *Twelve Feasts*
No. 53 London, Victoria and Albert Museum, *Feast Cycle Fragment*
No. 54 Athens, Benaki Museum, *Feast Cycle Fragment*
No. 55 Cherson, Museum, *Nativity*
No. 56 Cherson, Museum, *Ascension*
No. 57 Paris, Cabinet des Médailles, *Nativity Fragment*
No. 58 Athens, Benaki Museum, *Passion Cycle Fragment*
No. 59 Baltimore, Walters Art Gallery, *Passion Cycle Fragment*
No. 60 New York, Metropolitan Museum, *Passion Cycle Fragment*
No. 61 Cleveland, Museum of Art, *Passion Cycle Fragment*
No. 62 Kiti, Cyprus, *Feast Cycle*
No. 63 Berlin, Staatliche Museen, *Feast Cycle Fragment*
No. 64 Athens, Benaki Museum, *Feast Cycle Fragment*
No. 65 Toronto, University of Toronto, *Feast Cycle Fragment*
No. 66 Herakleion, Crete, Historical Museum, *Feast Cycle Fragment*
No. 67 Washington, D.C., Dumbarton Oaks, *Ascension*
No. 68 Princeton University, Art Museum, *Chairete*
No. 69 Berlin, Staatliche Museen, *Prophets*
No. 70 Leningrad, Hermitage, *Soldiers* (?)
No. 71 Chios, Archaeological Museum, *Koimesis*
No. 72 Location Unknown, *Koimesis*
No. 73 Location Unknown, *Pentecost*
No. 74 Berlin, Staatliche Museen, *Head of Constantine* (?)
No. 75 Paris, Cabinet des Médailles, *Staurotheque*: *Angel*
No. 76 Nikosia, Cyprus Museum, *Crucifixion*
No. 77 Stockholm, Statens Historiska Museum, *Crucifixion*
No. 78 Location Unknown, *Crucifixion*
No. 79 Paris, Cabinet des Médailles, *Crucifixion*
No. 80 London, Victoria and Albert Museum, *Hodegetria*
No. 82 Belgrade, National Museum, *Virgin Hagiosoritissa*
No. 83 Athens, Benaki Museum, *Fragment of an Icon*
No. 84 Berlin, Staatliche Museen, *Virgin*
No. 85 Location Unknown, *Archangel*
No. 86 Athens, Benaki Museum, *St. John*
No. 87 Paris, Cabinet des Médailles, *Solomon*
No. 88 Washington, D.C., Dumbarton Oaks, *St. Nicholas*

No. 89 Location Unknown, *Two Saints*
No. 90 Kiev, City Museum, *Medical Saints*
No. 91 Hamburg, Museum für Kunst und Gewerbe, *Deesis*
No. 92 London, British Museum, *Virgin orans*
No. 93 Paris, Cabinet des Médailles, *Military Saint*
No. 94 Leningrad, Hermitage, *Christ Pantokrator*
No. 95 Moscow, Historical Museum, *Man of Sorrows*
No. 96 Paris, Cabinet des Médailles, *St. Nicholas*
No. 97 Nikosia, Cyprus Museum, *St. Nicholas*
No. 98 Nikosia, Cyprus Museum, *St. John Chrysostomos* (?)
No. 99 Athens, Benaki Museum, *St. Demetrios*
No. 100 Berlin, Staatliche Museen, *SS. George and Theodore*
No. 101 Toronto, University of Toronto, *Virgin and Child*
No. 102 Mdina, Malta, Cathedral Museum, *Reliquary*
No. 103 Bologna, Museo Civico Archeologico, *Two Wings of a Triptych*
No. 104 Athens, Benaki Museum, *Center of Triptych: Annunciation*
No. 105 Athens, Benaki Museum, *Archangel Michael*
No. 106 Vatican, Museo Sacro, *Pantokrator*
No. 107 Vatican, Museo Sacro, *SS. Demetrios and Theodore/St. Michael and Daniel*
No. 108 Paris, Cabinet des Médailles, *Virgin orans*
No. 109 Moscow, Historical Museum, *Virgin orans*
No. 110 Paris, Louvre, *Archangel Michael*
No. 111 Berlin, Staatliche Museen, *St. John the Baptist*
No. 112 London, British Museum, *Christ Emmanuel*
No. 113 Toronto, University of Toronto, *Christ Emmanuel*
No. 114 Cleveland, Museum of Art, *Christ Emmanuel*
No. 115 Mt. Athos, Xenophontos, *Transfiguration*
No. 116 Richmond, Virginia Museum, *Transfiguration*
No. 117 London, British Museum, *Crucifixion*
No. 118 Vatican, Museo Sacro, *Passion Scenes*
No. 119 Athens, Benaki, *St. Nicholas*
No. 120 Vatican, Museo Sacro, *St. Nicholas*
No. 121 Cologne, Schnütgen Museum, *St. Nicholas*
No. 122 Belgrade, Museum of Decorative Arts, *St. Nicholas/St. Michael*
No. 123 Princeton University, Art Museum, *Triptych Wing*
No. 124 Moscow, Kremlin Armory, *St. Demetrios*
No. 125 Florence, Museo Nazionale del Bargello, *St. George*
No. 126 Mt. Athos, Vatopedi, *Virgin/Military Saints*
No. 127 Paris, Collection Marquis de Ganay, *St. Demetrios*
No. 128 Paris, Cabinet des Médailles, *Military Saint*
No. 129 New York, Art Market, *St. Theodore*
No. 130 Paris, Louvre, *St. Demetrios*
No. 131 Mt. Athos, Xeropotamu, *Panagiarion*
No. 132 Mt. Athos, Panteleimon, *Panagiarion*
No. 133 Berlin, Staatliche Museen, *Enthroned Virgin*
No. 134 London, British Museum, *Virgin and Child*
No. 135 Padua, Cathedral Treasury, *Christ Pantokrator*
No. 136 Location Unknown, *Archangel Michael*
No. 137 London, Roper Collection, *St. Demetrios*

No. 138	Washington, D.C., Dumbarton Oaks, *St. George*
No. 139	Location Unknown, *St. Demetrios*
No. 140	Vienna, Kunsthistorisches Museum, *St. George*
No. 141	Vatican, Museo Sacro, *St. Basil*
No. 142	Sofia, National Museum, *St. Demetrios*
No. 143	Vienna, Kunsthistorisches Museum, *St. George*
No. 144	Herakleion, Crete, Historical Museum, *St. Theodore*
No. 145	Moscow, Tretjakov Gallery, *Daniel*
No. 146	Paris, Louvre, *St. John the Theologian*
No. 147	New York, Metropolitan Museum, *Christ Antiphonetes*
No. 148	Cleveland, Museum of Art, *Fragment of a Crucifixion*
No. 149	Mt. Athos, Vatopedi, *Twelve Feasts*
No. 150	Location Unknown, *Entry into Jerusalem*
No. 151	Moscow, Historical Museum, *Ascension*
No. 152	Paris, Cabinet des Médailles, *Raising of Lazarus*
No. 153	London, British Museum, *Scene from the Passion*
No. 154	Athens, Benaki Museum, *Presentation in the Temple*
No. 155	Baltimore, Walters Art Gallery, *Pantokrator and Feasts*
No. 156	Cologne, Schnütgen Museum, *Hodegetria and Feasts*
No. 157	Baltimore, Walters Art Gallery, *Crucifixion and Feasts*
No. 158	London, British Museum, *Feast Cycle Fragment: Nativity*
No. 159	Ohrid, Treasury of St. Clement, *Twelve Feasts*
No. 160	Sinai, St. Catherine's Monastery, *Hodegetria and Feasts*
No. 161	Moscow, Historical Museum, *Feast Cycle Fragment*
No. 162	Berlin, Staatliche Museen, *Feast Cycle Fragment: Nativity*
No. 163	Berlin, Staatliche Museen, *Anastasis*
No. 164	Vatican, Museo Sacro, *Pentecost*
No. 165	Baltimore, Walters Art Gallery, *St. Gregory the Theologian*
No. 166	Paris, Cabinet des Médailles, *Pectoral Cross*
No. 167	Mt. Sinai, St. Catherine's Monastery, *Crucifixion*
No. 168	New York, Metropolitan Museum, *Christ, Feasts and Saints*
No. 169	Location Unknown, *Three Medical Saints*
No. 170	Vatican, Museo Sacro, *Christ Enthroned*
No. 171	Athens, Benaki Museum, *Koimesis*
No. 172	Berlin, Staatliche Museen, *Deesis*
No. 173	Vatican, Museo Sacro, *Crucifixion*
No. 174	Moscow, Kremlin Armory, *John the Baptist*
Appendix	
A-1	Athens, Benaki Museum, *Christ Pantokrator*
A-2	Athens, Benaki Museum, *Deesis*
A-3	Athens, Benaki Museum, *Christ Enthroned/Anastasis* (?)
A-4	Athens, Benaki Museum, *Virgin and Child/Military Saint*
A-5	Athens, Benaki Museum, *Anastasis* (?)
A-6	Athens, Benaki Museum, *Virgin*
A-7	Athens, Byzantine Museum, *St. Nicholas*
A-7 I	Athens, Byzantine Museum, *Crucifixion*
A-8	Baltimore, Walters Art Gallery, *Virgin and Child/St. Nicholas*
A-9	Baltimore, Walters Art Gallery, *St. George Slaying the Dragon*

A-10 Baltimore, Walters Art Gallery, *Virgin*

A-11 Baltimore, Walters Art Gallery, *Virgin and Child*

A-12 Berlin, Staatliche Museen, *St. George Slaying the Dragon*

A-13 Berlin, Staatliche Museen, *St. Demetrios and St. George*

A-14 Braunschweig, Herzog-Anton-Ulrich Museum, *St. George* (?)

A-15 Corinth, Corinth Museum, *Christ Pantokrator*

A-15 I Ephesos, Ephesos Museum, *Church Fathers and Feast Scenes*

A-20 London, British Museum, *St. Nicholas*

A-21 London, British Museum, *Daniel/St. Marina*

A-22 London, British Museum, *Bust of a Saint/Cross*

A-23 London, British Museum, *Virgin and Child/Two Standing Saints*

A-24 London, British Museum, *St. George Slaying the Dragon*

A-25 London, Victoria and Albert Museum, *Virgin/The Dead Christ*

A-26 London, Victoria and Albert Museum, *Crucifixion/Instruments of the Passion*

A-27 London, Victoria and Albert Museum, *Deesis*

A-28 London, Victoria and Albert Museum, *Boar Hunt*

A-29 London, Victoria and Albert Museum, *St. Basil*

A-30 Madrid, Museo Lazaro Goldiano, *Virgin and Child*

A-32 Moscow, Kremlin Armory, *Presentation, Entry into Jerusalem, Crucifixion, Anastasis*

A-33 New York, Ruth Blumka Collection, *Bust of Christ/St. Nicholas*

A-34 New York, Ruth Blumka Collection, *St. Nicholas*

A-35 New York, Brooklyn Museum, *Bust of Christ*

A-35 I New York, Metropolitan Museum of Art, *Crucifixion*

A-36 Nikosia, Cyprus Museum, *Virgin and Child*

A-37 Nikosia, Cyprus Museum, *St. Peter*

A-38 Nikosia, Cyprus Museum, *Christ Emmanuel*

A-39 Nikosia, Cyprus Museum, *Hodegetria*

A-40 Niš, National Museum, *Bust of the Virgin*

A-41 Paris, Bibliothèque Nationale, *Christ Emmanuel*

A-42 Paris, Bibliothèque Nationale, *Virgin and Child/Archangel*

A-43 Paris, Bibliothèque Nationale, *The Dead Christ/St. John the Theologian*

A-44 Paris, Bibliothèque Nationale, *Christ on the Cross*

A-45 Paris, Bibliothèque Nationale, *Bust of a Saint*

A-46 Paris, Bibliothèque Nationale, *Female Saint/Old Testament King*

A-47 Paris, Bibliothèque Nationale, *Crucifixion*

A-48 Paris, Bibliothèque Nationale, *St. Marina*

A-50 Philadelphia, Philadelphia Museum of Art, *Anastasis*

A-51 Recklinghausen, Ikonenmuseum, *Standing Hodegetria and St. Nicholas*

A-52 Reggio, Museo Nazionale, *St. George*

A-53 Richmond, Virginia Museum, *St. Marina/Daniel*

A-55 Sinai, Monastery of St. Catherine, *Deesis/Two Standing Saints*

A-56 Sofia, National Archaeological Museum, *St. George*

A-57 Toronto, University of Toronto, *St. Nicholas/Cross*

A-57 I Toronto, University of Toronto, *Angel*

A-58 Vatican, Museo Sacro, *St. Demetrios*

A-59 Vatican, Museo Sacro, *Bust of Christ*

A-60 Vatican, Museo Sacro, *Virgin and Child/St. Michael*

A-60 I Veliko Tŭrnovo, Archaeological Institute and Museum of the Academy of Sciences, *Military Saint*

A-60 II	Veliko Tŭrnovo, Archaeological Institute and Museum of the Academy of Sciences, *Saint*
A-60 III	Veliko Tŭrnovo, Archaeological Institute and Museum of the Academy of Sciences, *Saint*
A-60 IV	Veliko Tŭrnovo, Archaeological Institute and Museum of the Academy of Sciences, *Church Father*
A-61	Venice, Scuola Grande di S. Rocco, Treasury, *Crucifixion and Feast Cycle*
A-62	Vologda, Regional Museum, *St. Eustathios Plakidas*
A-63	Present Location Unknown (Ex-Kouchakij Collection, New York), *Archangel*
A-64	Present Location Unknown (Ex-Hirsch Collection), *St. Peter/Incised Cross*

1. Vienna, Kunsthistorisches Museum, *Koimesis*

13. Paris, Cabinet des Médailles, *St. Nicholas*

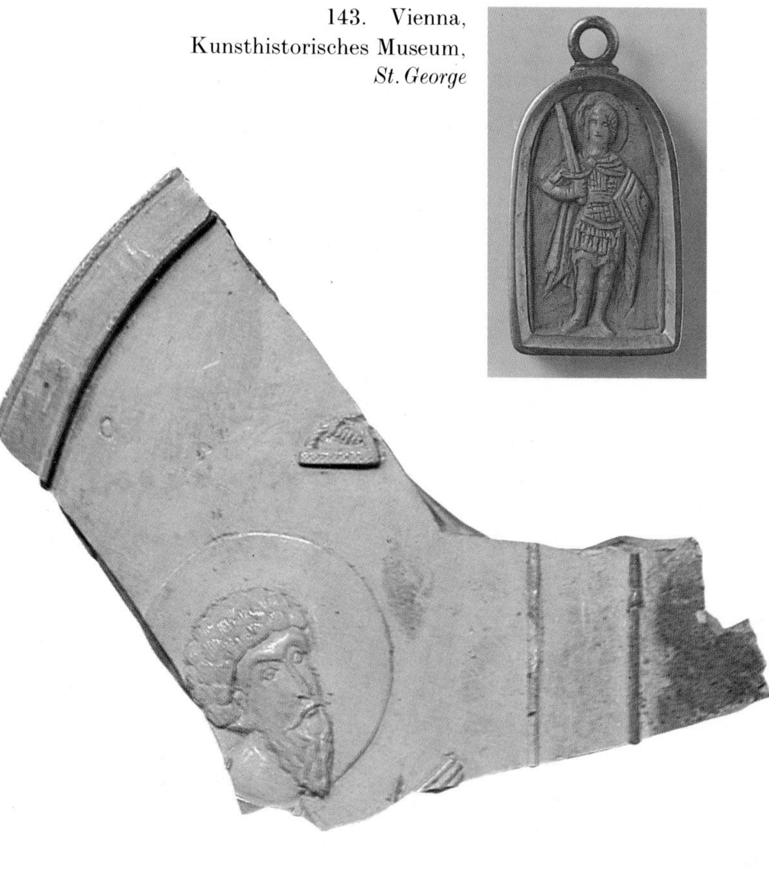

143. Vienna, Kunsthistorisches Museum, *St. George*

7. Cherson, Museum, *St. Theodore*

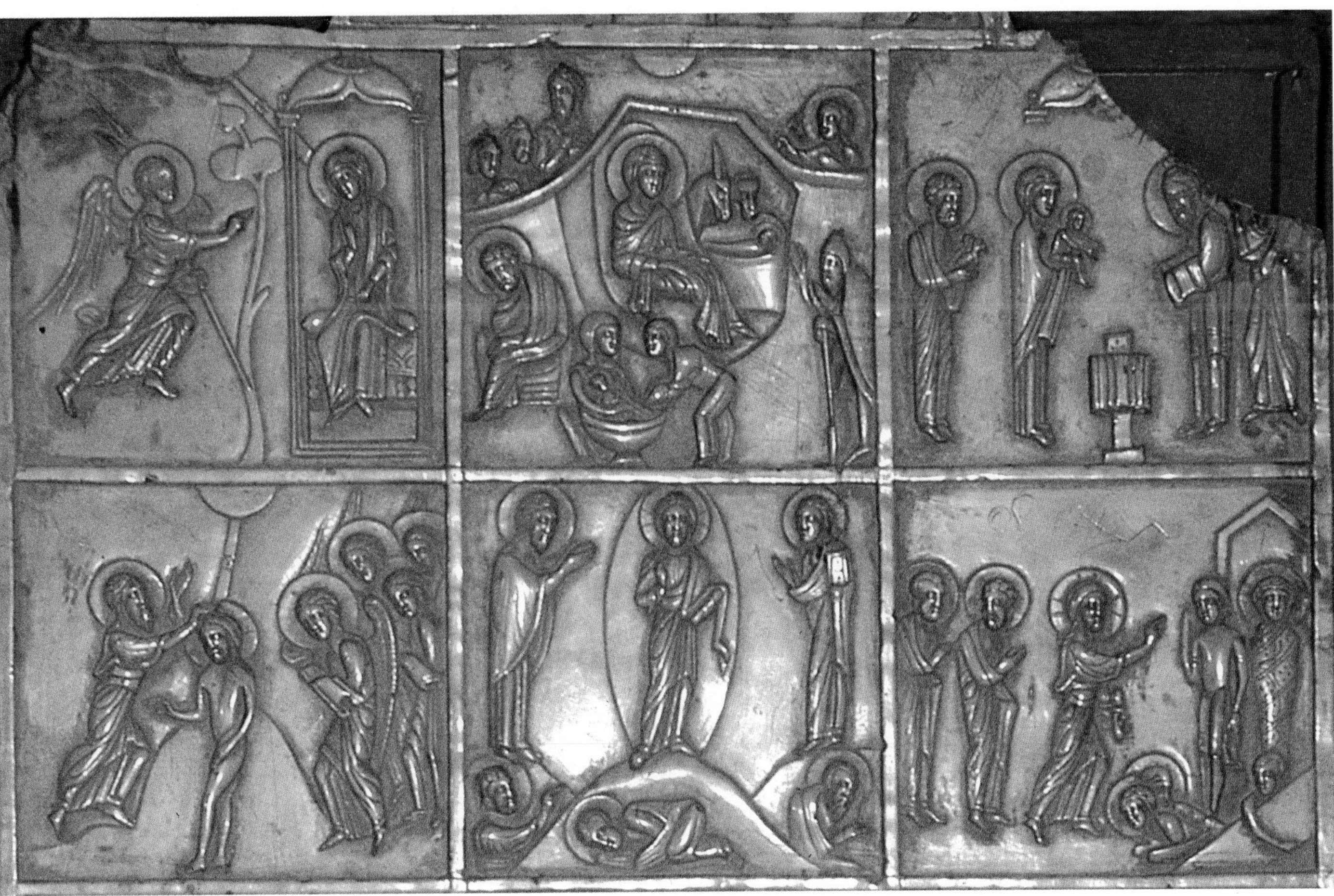

52. Toledo, Cathedral Treasury, *Twelve Feasts* (detail)

149. Mt. Athos, Vatopedi, *Twelve Feasts*

Examples of Steatite Crosses and Seals

1. Vienna, Kunsthistorisches Museum, *Koimesis*

2. Vatican, Museo Sacro, *Koimesis*

3. Paris, Coll. Marquis de Ganay, *Hetoimasia* (detail)

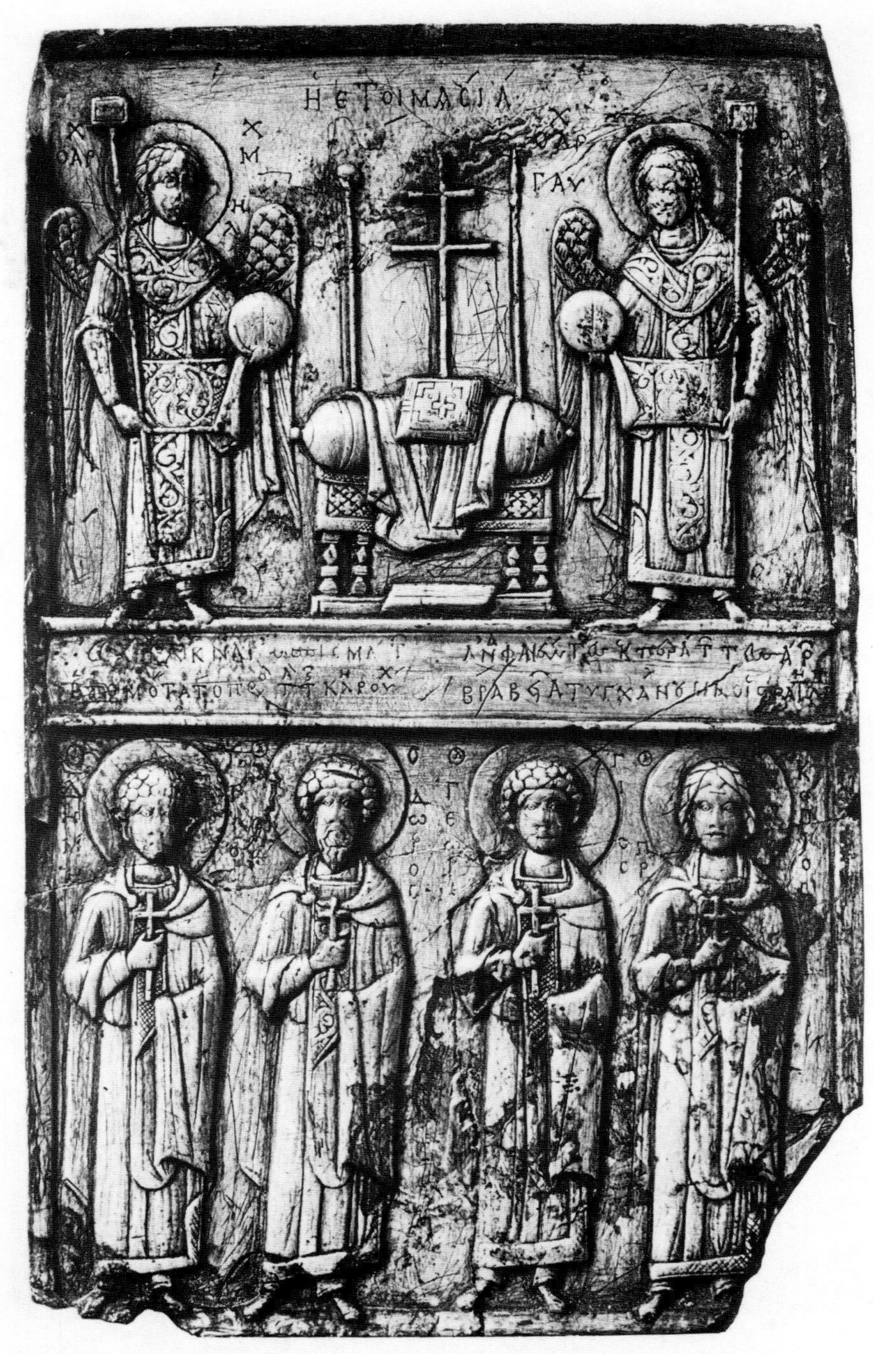

3. Paris, Coll. Marquis de Ganay, *Hetoimasia*

4. Leningrad, Hermitage, *Deesis and Saints*

PLATE 6

5. Washington, D.C., Dumbarton Oaks, *SS. George and Theodore*

7. Cherson, Museum, *St. Theodore*

9. Paris, Louvre, *Military Saint*

6. Vatican, Museo Sacro, *St. Theodore*

8. Mt. Athos, Vatopedi Monastery, *St. George*

10. Location Unknown, *St. Demetrios*

11. Paris, Louvre, *St. Demetrios*

12. Paris, Louvre, *St. John Chrysostomos*

13. Paris, Cabinet des Médailles, *St. Nicholas*

14. Mt. Sinai, St. Catherine's Monastery, *St. Nicholas* (reduced 9:10)

14. Mt. Sinai, St. Catherine's Monastery,
St. Nicholas

15. Cherson, Museum,
St. Demetrios

16. Richmond, Virginia Museum,
St. Demetrios

18. Paris, Cabinet des Médailles,
St. Nicholas

17. Toronto, University of Toronto,
Christ Emmanuel

19. Baltimore, Walters Art Gallery,
St. Panteleimon

20. Athens, Byzantine Museum,
Virgin

21. Cherson, Museum, *SS. Theodore, George, Demetrios*

22. Veliko Tŭrnovo, Museum,
SS. Theodore, George, Demetrios

24. Location Unknown,
Deesis

23. Agara, Museum, *Military Saints*

25. Kiev, City Museum, *Military Saints*

24 a. Veliko Tŭrnovo, Museum, *St. Theodore*

26. Princeton University, Art Museum, *Military Saint*

27. Veliko Tŭrnovo, Museum, *Three Military Saints*

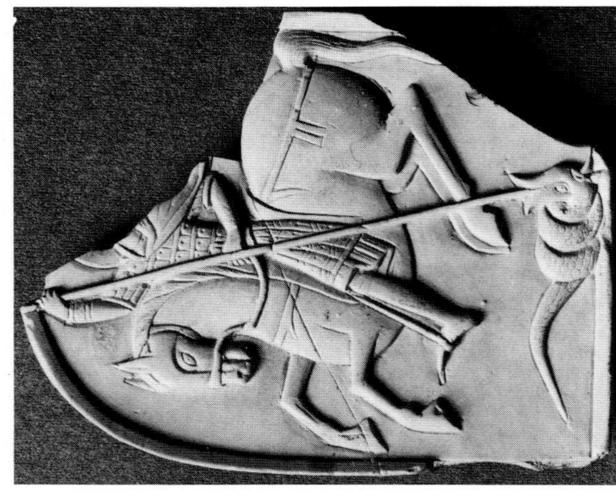

29. Baltimore, Walters Art Gallery, *St. George*

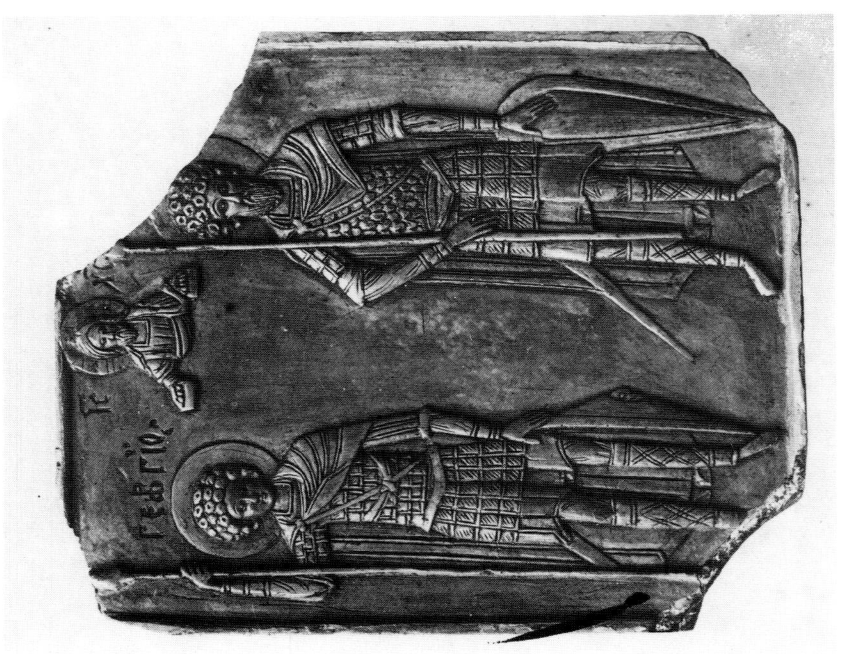

28. Moscow, Historical Museum, *SS. George and Theodore*

30. Fiesole, Museo Bandini, *Archangel Gabriel*

31. Stuttgart, Württenberg. Landesmuseum, *Virgin and Child*

32. Cleveland, Museum of Art, *Virgin and Child*

33. Florence, Mus. Naz. del Bargello, *Virgin and Child*

34. Vatican, Museo Sacro, *Virgin and Child*

35. Vatican, Museo Sacro, *St. Panteleimon* (reduced 1:2)

35. Vatican, Museo Sacro, *St. Panteleimon*

PLATE 22

36

37

38

39

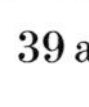

39 a

40

36. Athens, Benaki Museum, *St. Andrew.* — 37. London, British Museum, *St. Paul.* — 38. Berlin, Staatliche Museen, *St. Therapon.* — 39. Washington, D.C., Dumbarton Oaks, *Head of Saint.* — 40. Location Unknown, *Head of Saint*

41. Cherson, Museum, *Annunciation*

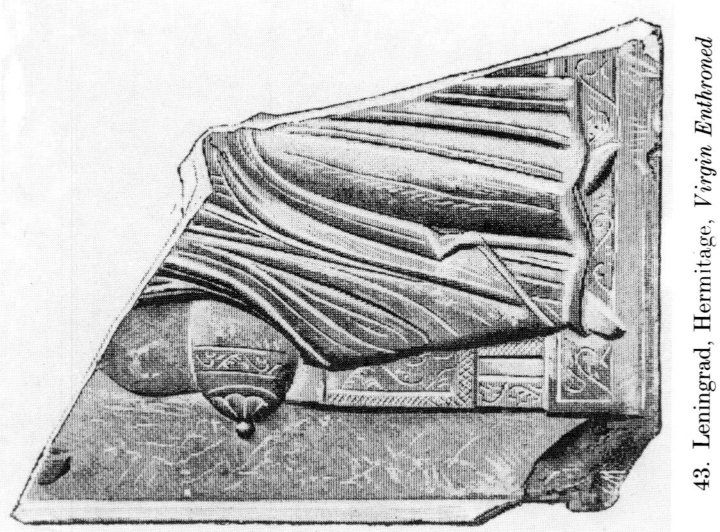

43. Leningrad, Hermitage, *Virgin Enthroned*

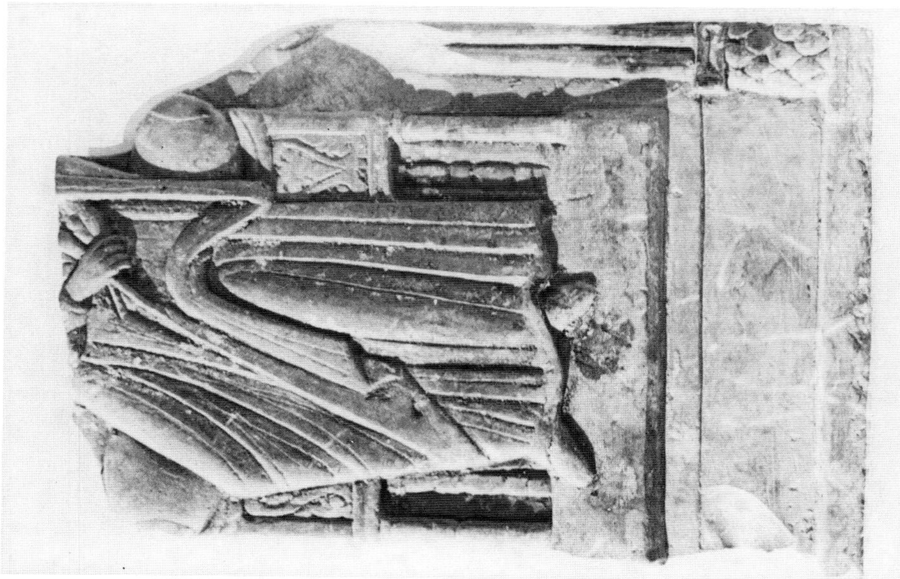

42. Istanbul, Archaeological Museum, *Annunciation*

PLATE 25

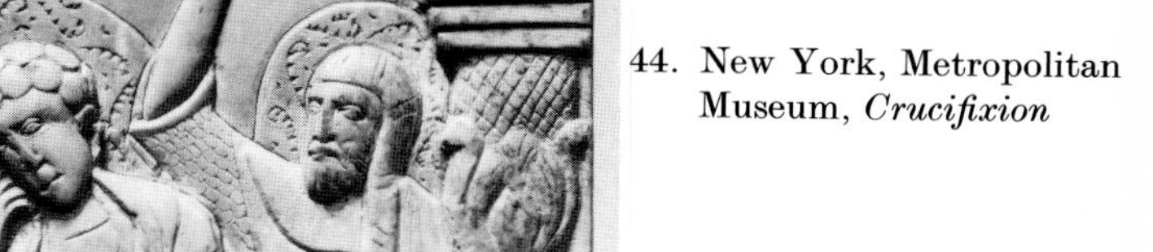

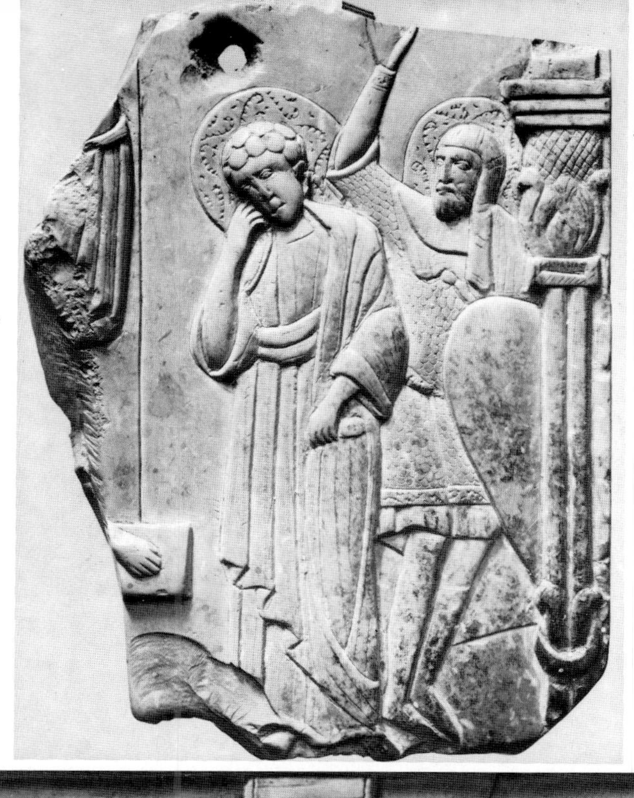

44. New York, Metropolitan Museum, *Crucifixion*

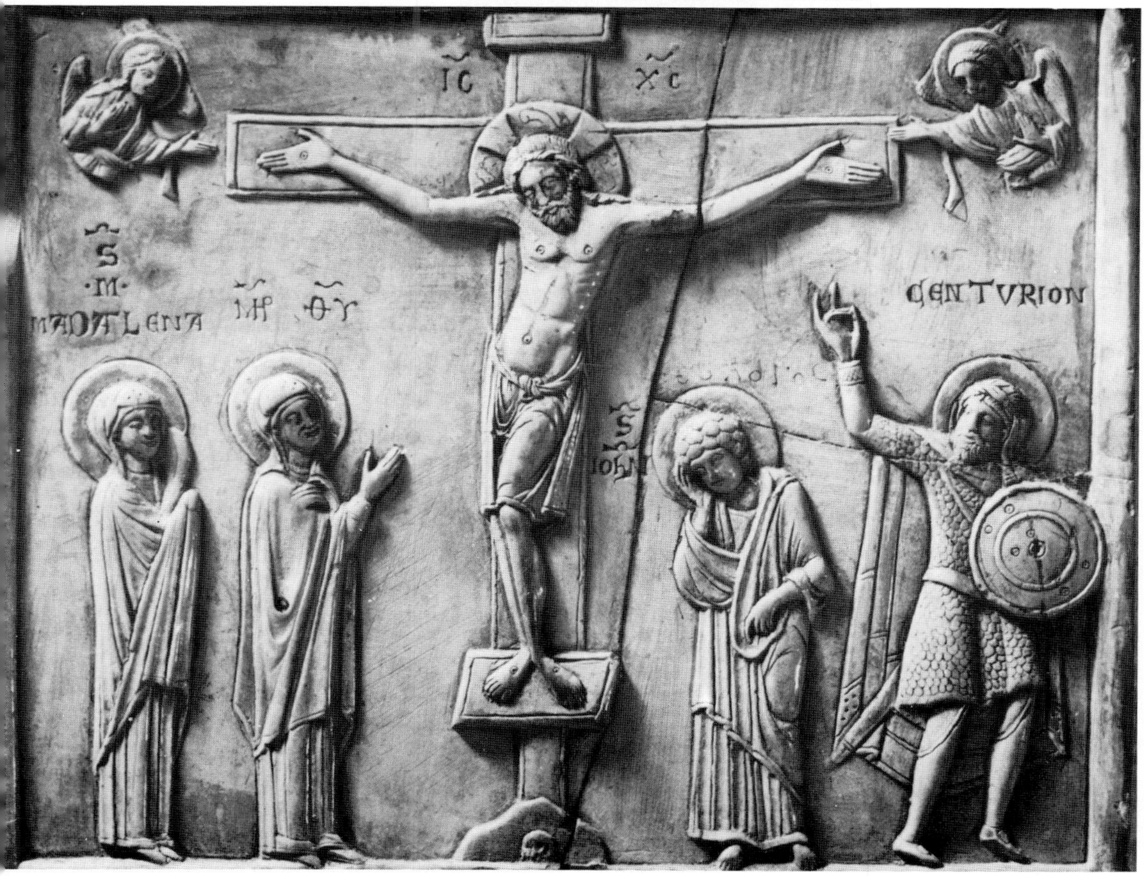

45. Leningrad, Hermitage, *Crucifixion* (detail)

45. Leningrad, Hermitage, *Crucifixion and Entombment* (reduced 8.5: 10)

45. Leningrad, Hermitage, *Entombment* (detail)

46. Syracuse, Palace of Archbishop, *Staurotheque*

47. Paris, Cabinet des Médailles, *Staurotheque*

48. Thasos, Museum, *Deesis*

51. Toronto, University of Toronto, *Saints*

49. Baltimore, Walters Art Gallery, *Crucifixion* (?)

50. New York, Metropolitan Museum, *Presentation in the Temple*

52. Toledo, Cathedral Treasury, *Twelve Feasts* (reduced 2:3)

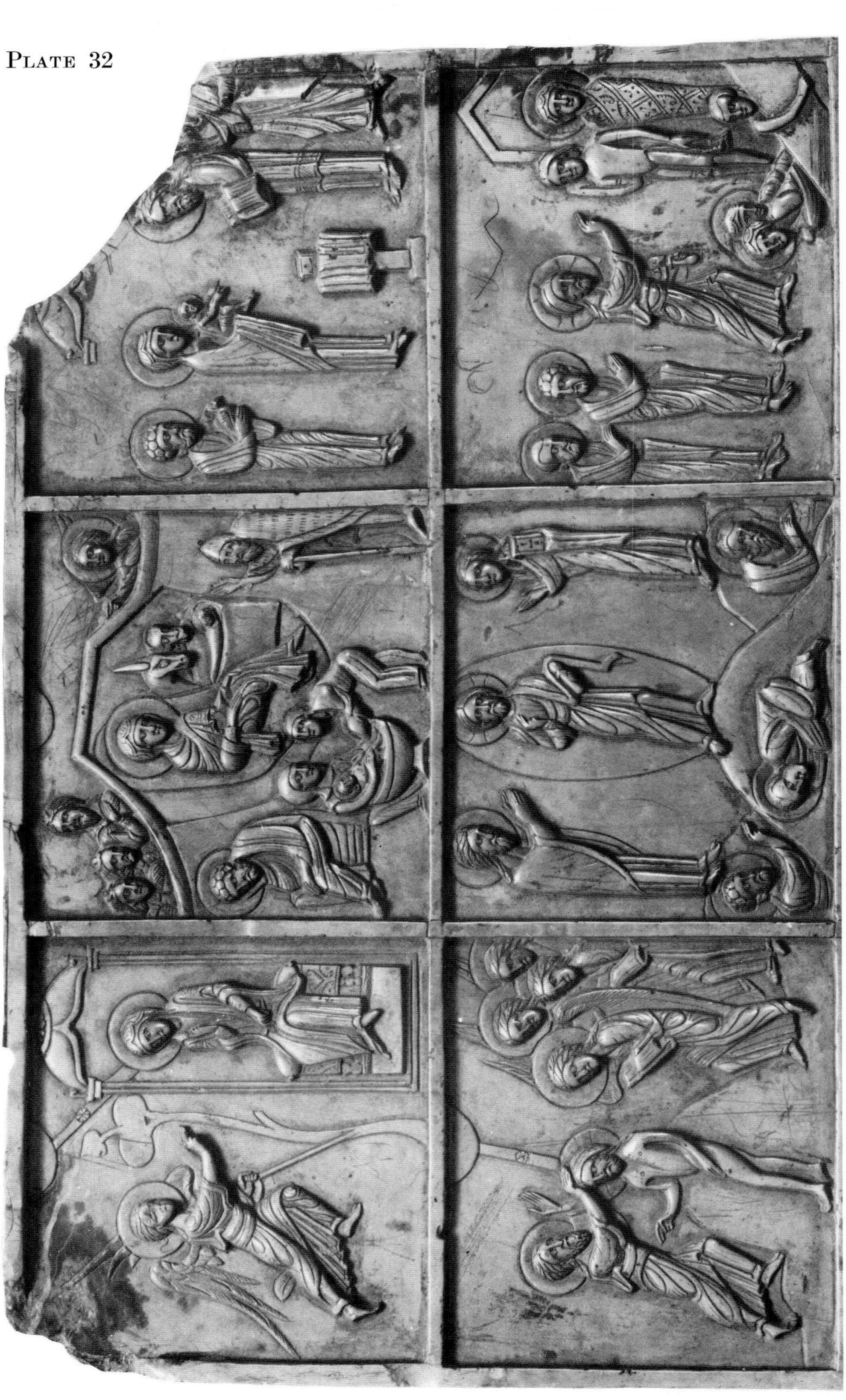

52. Toledo, Cathedral Treasury, *Twelve Feasts* (upper half)

52. Toledo, Cathedral Treasury, *Twelve Feasts* (lower half)

53. London, Victoria and Albert Museum, *Feast Cycle Fragment*

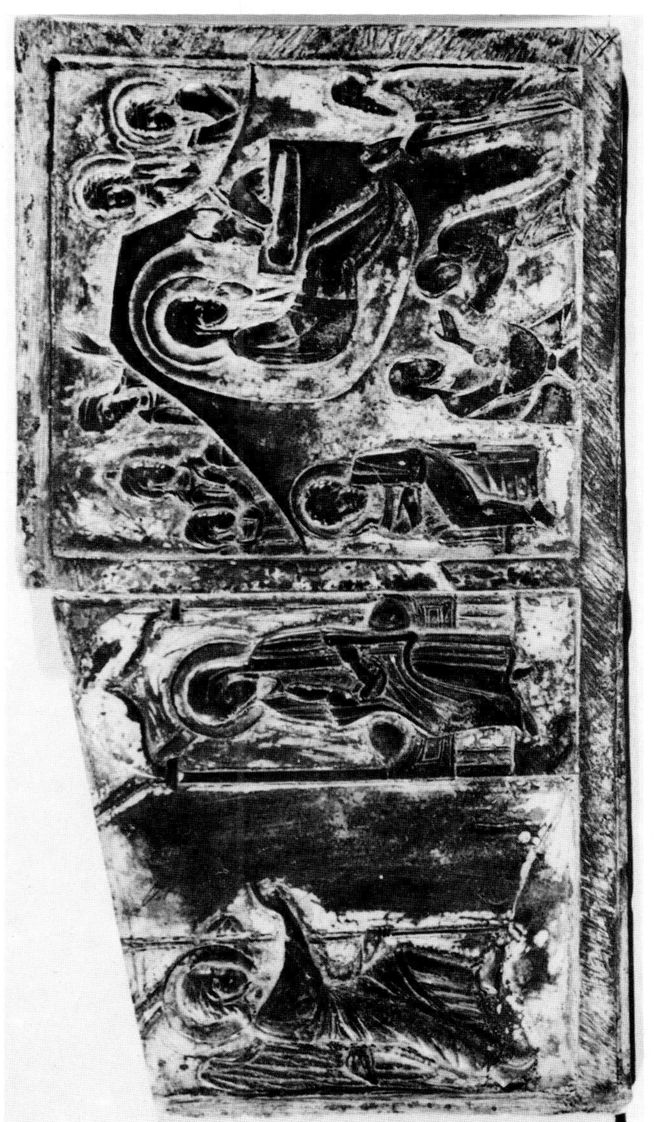

54. Athens, Benaki Museum, *Feast Cycle Fragment*

55. Cherson, Museum, *Nativity*

56. Cherson, Museum, *Ascension*

57. Paris, Cabinet des Médailles, *Nativity Fragment*

58. Athens, Benaki Museum, *Passion Cycle Fragment*

59. Baltimore, Walters Art Gallery, *Passion Cycle Fragment*

60. New York, Metropolitan Museum, *Passion Cycle Fragment*

61. Cleveland, Museum of Art, *Passion Cycle Fragment*

63. Berlin, Staatliche Museen, *Feast Cycle Fragment*

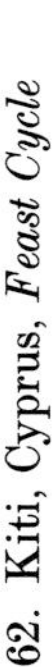

62. Kiti, Cyprus, *Feast Cycle*

64. Athens, Benaki Museum, *Feast Cycle Fragment*

65. Toronto, University of Toronto, *Feast Cycle Fragment*

66. Herakleion, Crete, Historical Museum, *Feast Cycle Fragment*

67. Washington, D. C., Dumbarton Oaks, *Ascension*

68. Princeton University, Art Museum, *Chairete*

69. Berlin, Staatliche Museen, *Prophets*

70. Leningrad, Hermitage, *Soldiers* (?)

PLATE 42

72. Location Unknown, *Koimesis*

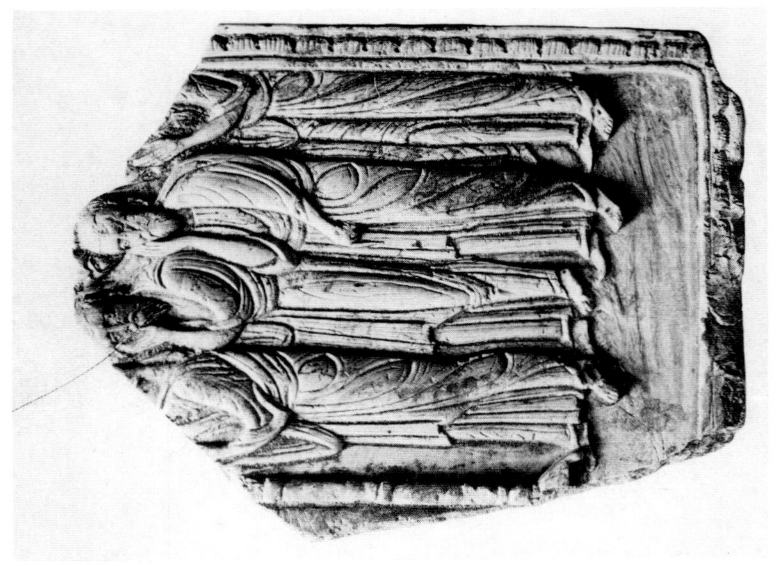

71. Chios, Archaeological Museum, *Koimesis*

75. Paris, Cabinet des Médailles, *Staurotheque: Angel*

73. Location Unknown, *Pentecost*

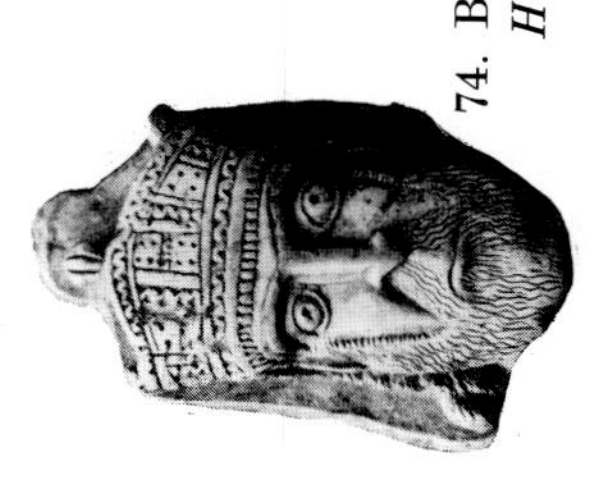

74. Berlin, Staatliche Museen, *Head of Constantine* (?)

78. Location Unknown, *Crucifixion*

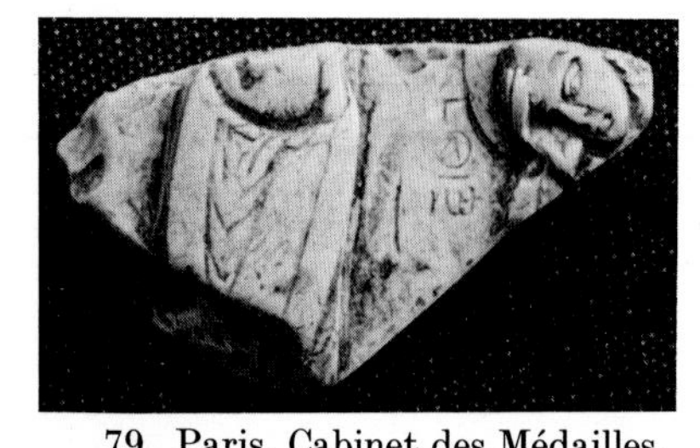

79. Paris, Cabinet des Médailles, *Crucifixion*

76. Nikosia, Cyprus Museum, *Crucifixion*

77. Stockholm, Statens Historiska Museum, *Crucifixion*

80. London, Victoria and Albert Museum, *Hodegetria*

82. Belgrade, National Museum, *Virgin Hagiosoritissa*

83

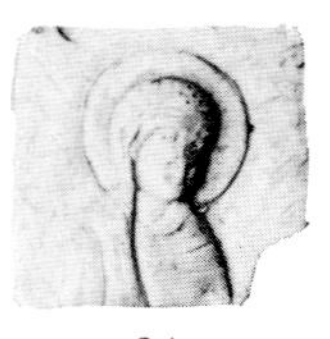

84

85

86

87

83. Athens, Benaki Museum, *Fragment of an Icon.* — 84. Berlin, Staatliche Museen, *Virgin.* — 85. Location Unknown, *Archangel.* — 86. Athens, Benaki Museum, *St. John.* — 87. Paris, Cabinet des Médailles, *Solomon*

88. Washington, D.C., Dumbarton Oaks, *St. Nicholas*

89. Location Unknown, *Two Saints*

90. Kiev, City Museum, *Medical Saints*

91. Hamburg, Museum für Kunst und Gewerbe, *Deesis*

92. London, British Museum, *Virgin orans*

93. Paris, Cabinet des Médailles, *Military Saint*

94. Leningrad, Hermitage, *Christ Pantokrator*

95. Moscow, Historical Museum, *Man of Sorrows*

96. Paris, Cabinet des Médailles, *St. Nicholas*

97. Nikosia, Cyprus Museum,
St. Nicholas

98. Nikosia, Cyprus Museum,
St. John Chrysostomos (?)

99. Athens, Benaki Museum,
St. Demetrios

100. Berlin, Staatliche Museen,
SS. George and Theodore

101. Toronto, University of Toronto,
Virgin and Child

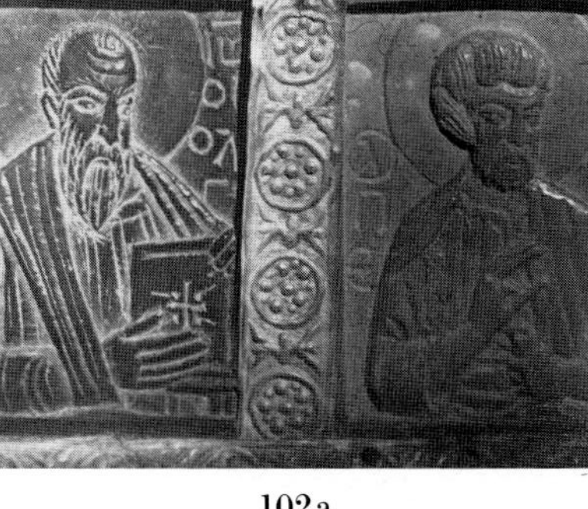

102a

102b

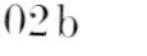

102c

102. Mdina, *Reliquary* (details): a) *SS. Paul, Basil, John, Peter*; b) *Crucifixion*; c) *SS. Cosmas and Damian, St. Zosimas and Mary of Egypt, St. Sabas*

103. Bologna, Museo Civico Archeologico, *Two Wings of a Triptych*

104. Athens, Benaki Museum, *Center of Triptych: Annunciation*

105. Athens, Benaki Museum, *Archangel Michael*

106. Vatican, Museo Sacro, *Pantokrator*

107. Vatican, Museo Sacro, *SS. Demetrios and Theodore/St. Michael and Daniel*

109. Moscow, Historical Museum, *Virgin orans*

108. Paris, Cabinet des Médailles, *Virgin orans*

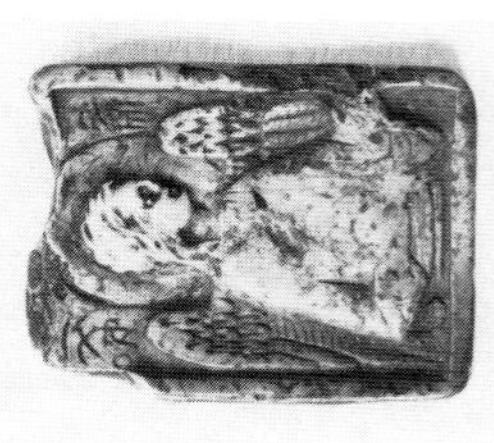

110. Paris, Louvre, *Archangel Michael*

111. Berlin, Staatliche Museen, *St. John the Baptist*

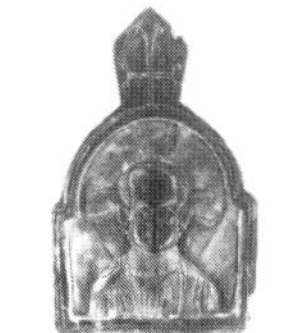

112. London, British Museum, *Christ Emmanuel*

113. Toronto, University of Toronto, *Christ Emmanuel*

114. Cleveland, Museum of Art, *Christ Emmanuel*

115. Mt. Athos, Xenophontos, *Transfiguration*

117. London, British Museum, *Crucifixion*

116. Richmond, Virginia Museum, *Transfiguration*

118. Vatican, Museo Sacro, *Passion Scenes*

119. Athens, Benaki, *St. Nicholas*

120. Vatican, Museo Sacro, *St. Nicholas*

123 a

121

122 a

122 b

123 b

121. Cologne, Schnütgen Museum, *St. Nicholas.* — 122. Belgrade, Museum of Decorative Arts, *St. Nicholas/St. Michael.* — 123. Princeton University, Art Museum, *Triptych Wing*

124. Moscow, Kremlin Armory, *St. Demetrios* (reduced 8.5:10)

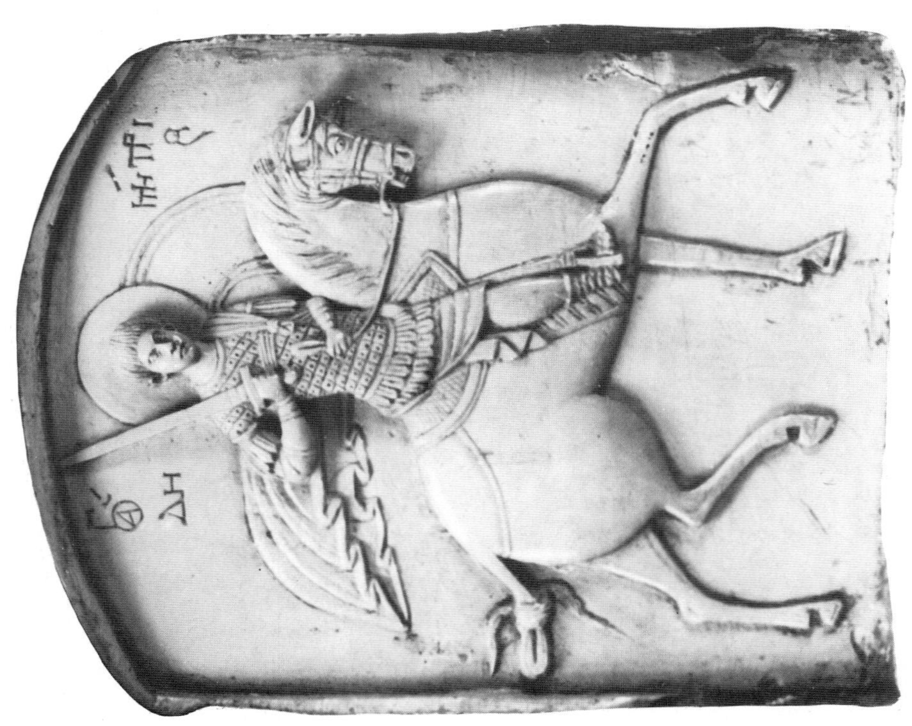

124. Moscow, Kremlin Armory, *St. Demetrios*

125. Florence, Museo Nazionale del Bargello, *St. George*

126. Mt. Athos, Vatopedi, two-sided icon, *Virgin/Military Saints*

127. Paris, Collection Marquis de Ganay, *St. Demetrios*

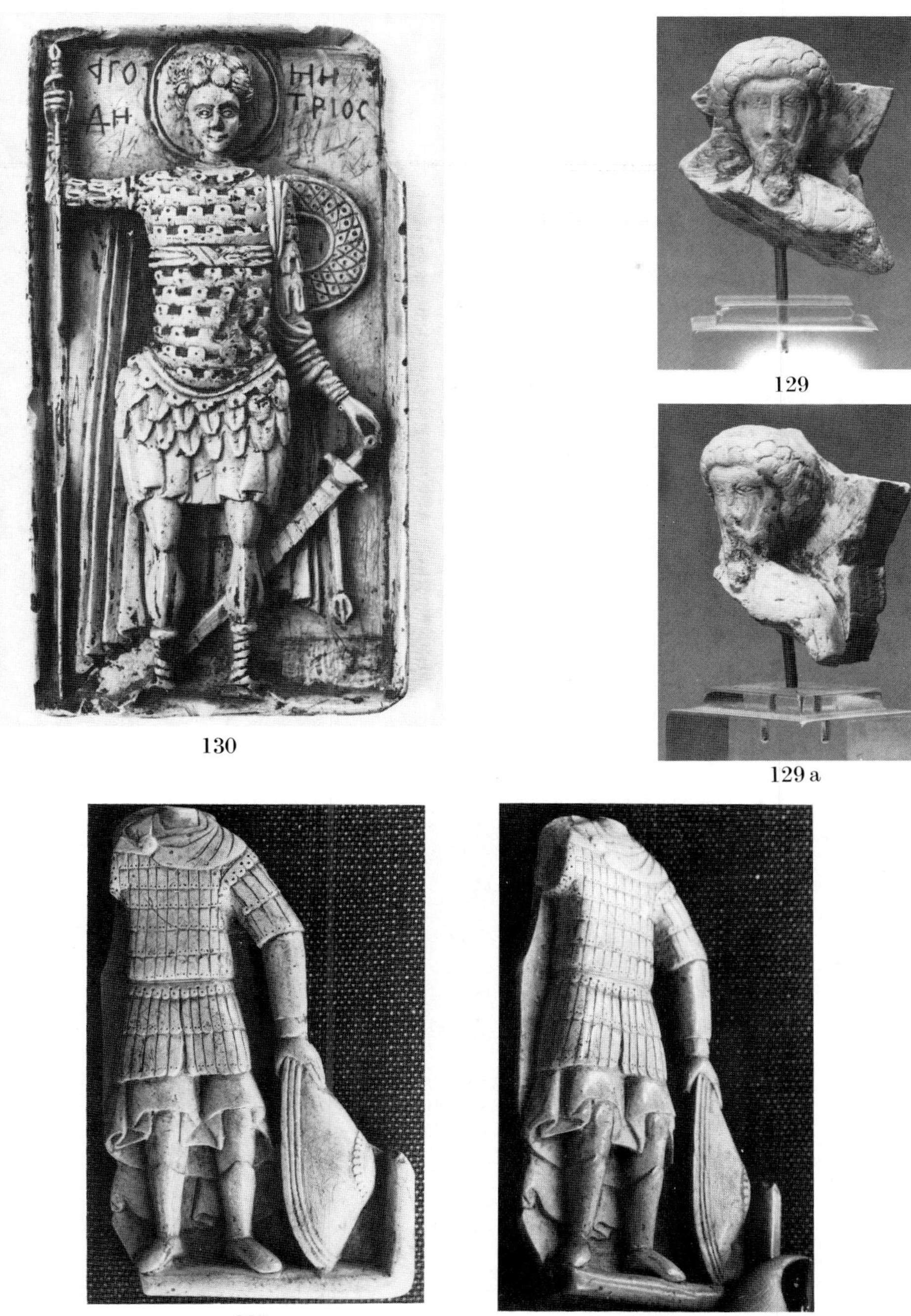

130

129

129 a

128

128 a

128. Paris, Cabinet des Médailles, *Military Saint.* — 129. New York, Art Market, *St. Theodore.* — 130. Paris, Louvre, *St. Demetrios*

131. Mt. Athos, Xeropotamu, *Panagiarion*

132. Mt. Athos, Panteleimon, *Panagiarion*

133. Berlin, Staatliche Museen,
Enthroned Virgin

134. London, British Museum,
Virgin and Child

135. Padua, Cathedral Treasury,
Christ Pantokrator

136. Location Unknown,
Archangel Michael

137 138 139

143 140 141

142

137. London, Roper Collection, *St. Demetrios.* — 138. Washington, D. C., Dumbarton Oaks, *St. George.* — 139. Location Unknown, *St. Demetrios.* — 140. Vienna, Kunsthistorisches Museum, *St. George.* — 141. Vatican, Museo Sacro, *St. Basil.* — 142. Sofia, National Museum, *St. Demetrios.* — 143. Vienna, Kunsthistorisches Museum, *St. George*

144. Herakleion, Crete, Historical Museum, *St. Theodore.* — 145. Moscow, Tretjakov Gallery, *Daniel.* — 146. Paris, Louvre, *St. John the Theologian.* — 147. New York, Metropolitan Museum, *Christ Antiphonetes.* — 148. Cleveland, Museum of Art, *Fragment of a Crucifixion*

149. Mt. Athos, Vatopedi, *Twelve Feasts* (reduced 4:5)

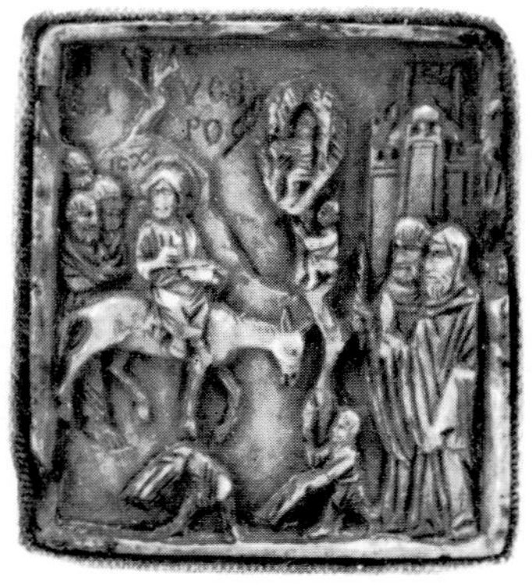

PLATE 70

150

151

152

153

154

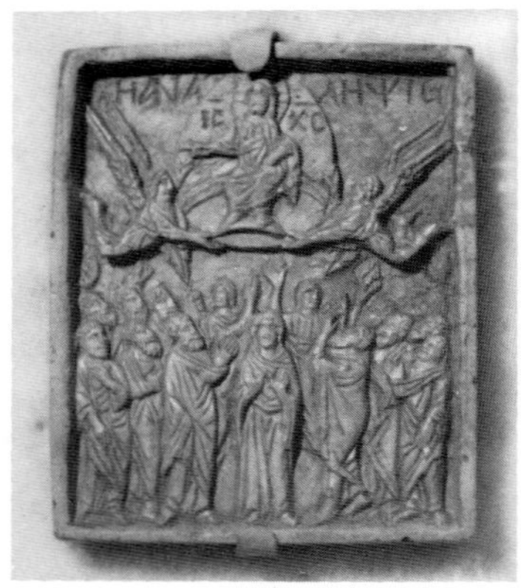

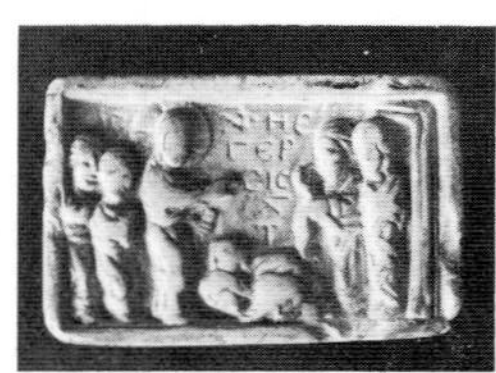

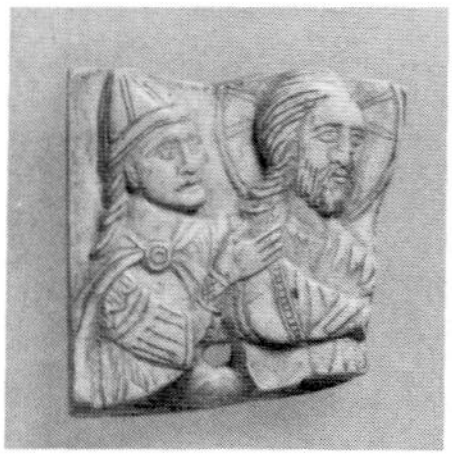

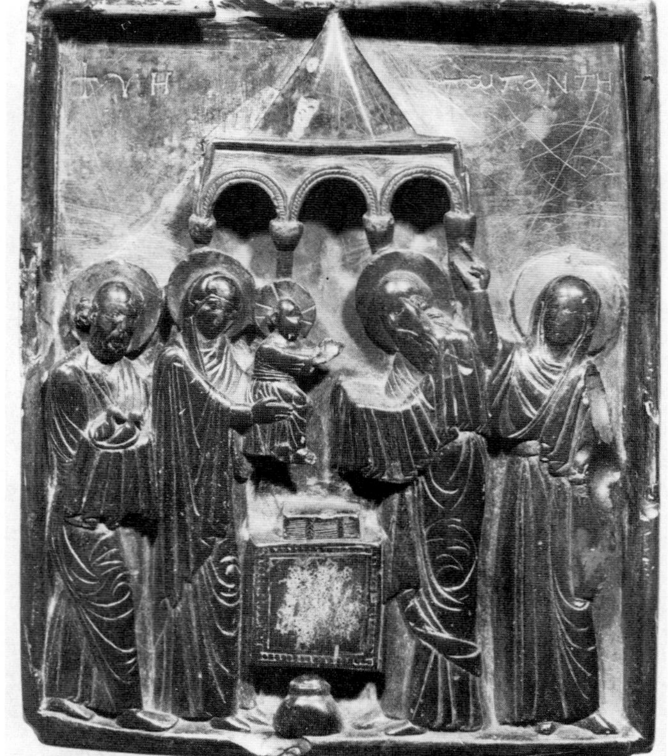

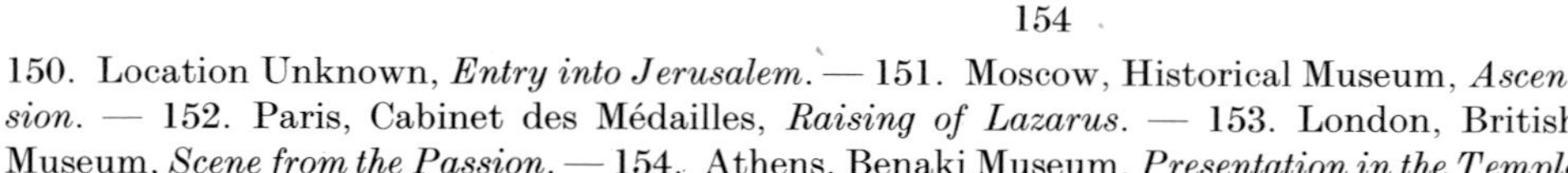

150. Location Unknown, *Entry into Jerusalem*. — 151. Moscow, Historical Museum, *Ascension*. — 152. Paris, Cabinet des Médailles, *Raising of Lazarus*. — 153. London, British Museum, *Scene from the Passion*. — 154. Athens, Benaki Museum, *Presentation in the Temple*

156. Cologne, Schnütgen Museum, *Hodegetria and Feasts*

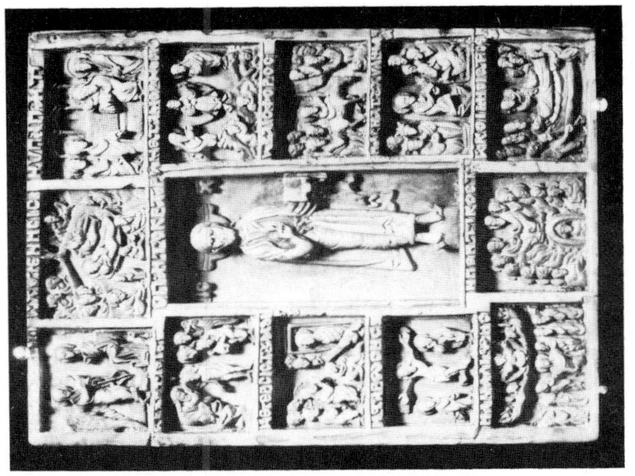

155. Baltimore, Walters Art Gallery, *Pantokrator and Feasts*

157

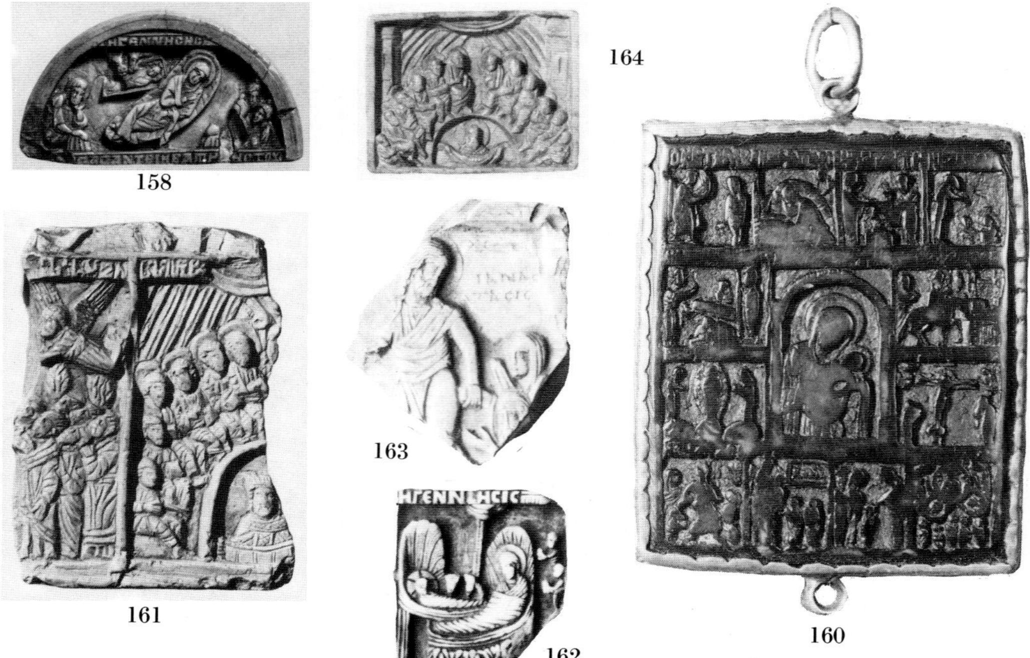

158

164

161

163

162

160

157. Baltimore, Walters Art Gallery, *Crucifixion and Feasts*. — 158. London, British Museum, *Feast Cycle Fragment: Nativity*. — 160. Mt. Sinai, St. Catherine's Monastery, *Hodegetria and Feasts*. — 161. Moscow, Historical Museum, *Feast Cycle Fragment*. — 162. Berlin, Staatliche Museen, *Feast Cycle Fragment: Nativity*. — 163. Berlin, Staatliche Museen, *Anastasis*. — 164. Vatican, Museo Sacro, *Pentecost*

159

165

166

166 a

159. Ohrid, Treasury of St. Clement, *Twelve Feasts.* — 165. Baltimore, Walters Art Gallery, *St. Gregory the Theologian.* — 166. Paris, Cabinet des Médailles, *Pectoral Cross*

168. New York, Metropolitan Museum, *Christ, Feasts and Saints*

167. Mt. Sinai, St. Catherine's Monastery, *Crucifixion*

169. Location unknown, *Three Medical Saints*

170. Vatican, Museo Sacro, *Christ Enthroned*

171. Athens, Benaki Museum, *Koimesis*

172. Berlin, Staatliche Museen, *Deesis*

173. Vatican, Museo Sacro, *Crucifixion*

174. Moscow, Kremlin Armory, *John the Baptist*

A-1. Athens, *Christ Pantokrator*

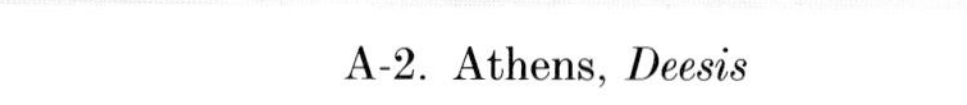

A-2. Athens, *Deesis*

A-3. Athens, *Christ Enthroned/Anastasis* (?)

A-4. Athens, *Virgin and Child/Military Saint*

A-5. Athens, *Anastasis* (?)

A-6. Athens, *Virgin*

A-7. Athens, *St. Nicholas*

A-7 I. Athens, *Crucifixion*

A-8 a. Baltimore, *Virgin and Child*

A-9. Baltimore, *St. George*

A-8 b. Baltimore, *St. Nicholas*

A-10. Baltimore, *Virgin*

A-11. Baltimore, *Virgin and Child*

A-12. Berlin, *St. George*

A-13. Berlin, *St. Demetrios and St. George*

A-15. Corinth,
Christ Pantokrator

A-15 I. Ephesos, *Church Fathers and Feast Scenes* (12th C.)

A-14. Braunschweig, *St. George* (?)

A-21. London, *Daniel/St. Marina*

A-23. London, *Virgin and Child/Saints*

A-20. London, *St. Nicholas*

A-22. London, *Saint/Cross*

A-24. London,
St. George

A-25. London, *Virgin/The Dead Christ*

A-26. London, *Crucifixion/Instruments of the Passion*

A-27. London, *Deesis*

A-28. London, *Boar hunt*

A-29. London, *St. Basil*

A-30. Madrid, *Virgin and Child*

A-32. Moscow, *Presentation, Entry into Jerusalem, Crucifixion, Anastasis*

A-33. New York, *Bust of Christ/St. Nicholas*

A-34. New York,
St. Nicholas

A-35. New York,
Bust of Christ

A-35 I. New York, *Crucifixion*

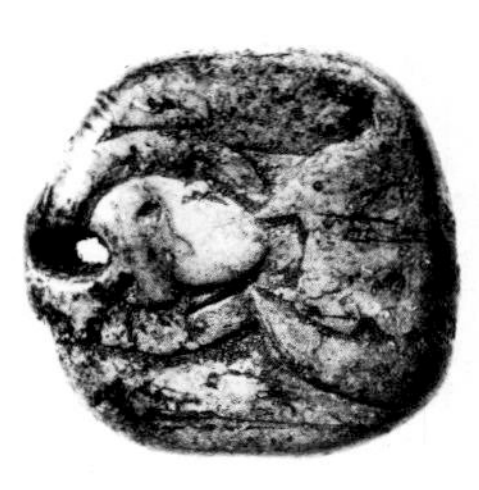

A-38. Nikosia, *Christ Emmanuel*

A-39. Nikosia, *Hodegetria*

A-37. Nikosia, *St. Peter*

A-36. Nikosia, *Virgin and Child*

A-40. Niš, *Bust of the Virgin*

A-41. Paris, *Christ Emmanuel*

A-42. Paris, *Virgin and Child/Archangel*

A-43. Paris, *The Dead Christ/St. John the Theologian*

A-44. Paris, *Christ on the Cross*

A-45. Paris, *Saint*

A-46. Paris, *Female Saint/Old Testament King*

A-48. Paris, *St. Marina*

A-47. Paris, *Crucifixion*

A-50. Philadelphia, *Anastasis*

A-52. Reggio, *St. George*

A-53. Richmond, *St. Marina/Daniel*

A-51. Recklinghausen, *Hodegetria and St. Nicholas*

A-56. Sofia, *St. George*

A-55. Sinai, *Deesis/Two Standing Saints*

A-57 I. Toronto, *Angel*

A-57. Toronto, *St. Nicholas/Cross*

A-58. Vatican, *St. Demetrios*

A-59. Vatican, *Bust of Christ*

A-60. Vatican, *Virgin and Child/St. Michael*

A-61. Venice, *Crucifixion and Feast Cycle*

A-60 IV. Veliko Tŭrnovo, *Church Father*

A-62. Vologda, *St. Eustathios Plakidas*

A-60 I. Veliko Tŭrnovo, *Military Saint*

A-60 II. Veliko Tŭrnovo, *Saint*

A-60 III. Veliko Tŭrnovo, *Saint*

A-64. Present Location Unknown, *St. Peter/Incised Cross*

A-63. Present Location Unknown, *Archangel*